Still Enough to Be Dreaming

Still Enough to Be Dreaming

Poems

Charlotte Hilary Matthews

Iris Press
Oak Ridge, Tennessee

Iris Press is an imprint of the Iris Publishing Group, Inc

www.irisbooks.com

Library of Congress Cataloging-in-Publication Data

Matthews, Charlotte Hilary, 1966-
Still enough to be dreaming : poems / Charlotte Hilary Matthews.
    p. cm.
ISBN-13: 978-0-916078-84-3 (pbk. : alk. paper)
I. Title.
PS3613.A8447S75 2007
811'.6—dc22

2007027313

Acknowledgments

Grateful acknowledgment is made to the following publications in which these poems first appeared.

Asheville Poetry Review: "Before the Summer Storm," "To See Things as They Are," "Alone on the Housetop"

Cave Wall: "Being Someone Else," "Evensong," "Exactitude"

Ecotone: "Not Telling Anything New"

Eclipse: "Field Guide to Confinement"

Hollins Critic: "Field Guide to Stillness"

Streetlight: "Hand Shadows on a Wall," "So The Snow Will Fall This Night"

storySouth: "Field Guide to Gentleness," "How To Claim Silence," "The Cancer Patient Dreams"

Spoon River Poetry Review: "In The Other Room My Daughter Plays with Her Dollhouse"

Virginia Quarterly Review: "To The Men Who Mow the County Graveyards," "Stablehand's Song"

Without friends who held my energy for me until I could it myself, this book would not have come to be. I am ever thankful to Cassandra Barnett, Cynthia Chase, Les and Susan Butchart, Linda Erday, Dick Harrington, Pam Gould, Evelyn Kitchin, Jill Gerard, Ron Rash and Kristin Sherman.

I am grateful to Dan Albergotti, Claire Bateman, Glenn Kessler and Ira Sadoff for their devoted reading of the poems.

I am indebted to my editor, Bob Cumming, for his patience and his acumen.

I would like to thank my oncologist, Dr. Gordon Morris, and all his capable staff for believing in me.

for Emma

Contents

III — Confinement

IV — Vanishing

V — Dreaming

Before a Summer Storm

My neighbor's mules
bray to each other.
One broke through the fence
and can't get back.
The other circles their small
pasture over and over.
Their sound like nothing
I have ever heard
but what I know separation to be:
unmistakable cry
across the riverbed.

I
Gentleness

Field Guide to Gentleness

A man sits the last four years
outside the gorilla cage watching
the eldest male swing between
branches of pale, uprooted trees.

The gorilla sits with his back
to the man who sits with his back
to me, every day on his folding chair,
every day the roar of tourist voices

reverberating off cinder walls,
every day his friend behind bars.
When the ape dies in early summer,
and the man stops coming to the zoo,

he explains for the radio:
Now I am the one in the cage.
How he is able to wake
each morning when even the trees

are holding their breath
remains a secret I will never know.
Like all great loves
this one ends in death.

Wait Until the Rain Stops

All at once I notice I'm standing
like my mother, looking straight
ahead in line at the bank,
left foot turned slightly to the side.
Or at the kitchen table, early summer,
as children chase a ball down the alley.
When it comes to a stop inches
from the storm drain, I exhale
the breath I've been holding
just like she would do
whenever tires squealed
at the corner light
and there wasn't a crash.
Sometimes I let myself
believe the woman
who talks to herself
at the covered bus stop
is my mother, but in another body.
When I see her, I look away
quick so she won't disappear.

Alone on the Housetop

She waits up nights, the cigarette's long
ash shredding in a perfect arc.
Traffic lessens, cars idling alone.
It might be she has forgotten what
she is waiting for—the light's rhythmic changing
a way to measure time, or a way out of time,
until it is any night, another city: somewhere
she lived as a child and could understand—
the hours fall into one another
and the eventual sunrise startles her
enough so at last she may find sleep.

Thinking from the Inside Out

It was what people intended to do that counted.
—William Maxwell

At the bank a man took tiny pieces
of paper out of his pocket and read them
under his breath just loud enough
for me to hear some of the words.
My mother set the kitchen timer even
when she was only boiling water,
as if afraid of forgetting what she couldn't see.

The day of her funeral it rained.
Outside Christ Church, the Saturday
traffic was congested because it was
the city, and January, and people
had to get out of the house for awhile.
But when I walked out of the atrium
and saw the wet black street
full of cars, it was unimaginable.

To See Things as They Are

In the field a horse stands
still enough to be dreaming,
the grasses all around have been
smoothed placid as ironed sheets
unfurled on a bed,
or the echo of bats in the dark.

What we do we do in silence
until it swells the way it did
for my brother walking up
the funeral home stairs
to identify our mother's body.

Inside his head, the knowledge
of what he would see:
shape without a name,
shape of a dim moth,
shape of a silken rock
the size of a swan's heart.

But late that night when he called,
I thought of all the moments
of salvation in our lives:
star of seeds in the center
of an apple cut horizontal
or the five doves
floating inside a sand dollar.
It just may be she found
a life that was, in some small
way, what she wanted, after all.

All I Need to Know

The imperfect tense in Greek
establishes a deed as going on,
incomplete at some time in the past.

The woman who lives by the highway
can tell your fortune, silently spread your hand
out flat, sulfur butterfly under glass,
pattern a riddle no one should know.
She tells of a girl who dreams
an injured doe steps right up to her.
The girl feels a strong heart beating,
and that changes everything.
It makes me think of all
the things we really miss.
The séance table tilts and leans,
the cabinet, where napkins are kept,
blows open, and my daughter, who is eight,
has developed a taste for pomegranates.
This makes me sore afraid.

Being Someone Else

What I learned from the spider web
is that we are invisible
until something touches us,
like the dew that made it brilliant
against the fallow pasture.
For dress up, my daughter
wants to be a pink fairy princess.

Off in the distance they
are making fire out of windfall,
piling sticks one on another
in hopes there will be light.
What she wants to be
is transparent, skirt of gossamer
with tiny shimmering stars.

What Is Near Pleases Us

The man cleaning fish down at the docks
is at work long past anyone's notice.
In the half-dark he knifes open the bellies,
each quick cut unencumbered,
his mind so absorbed in what he's doing
he appears to not need anyone
working on every evening as the light
becomes pale, then restless, then almost gone.

The first time I saw snow it was night.
Streetlights on the corner blurred through thick
air, each gauzy beam strewn behind like a comet.
My mother saw the world this way
whenever she took off her glasses:
the blue spruce in the neighbor's yard
became streaked as if she'd been crying.
But the work close-up, the book she was reading
or the needle threading, was clear and unswerving.
Her eyelids had light all through them.

The woman who keeps my daughter cracks walnuts
with a hammer on a smooth stone set in her lap.
Every afternoon since October she bends over
her work, leaning toward it,
picking each black nut from its hull.

Children's Teeth

The white-throated sparrow
out in the leaves sings—
O Sam Peabody, Sam Peabody, O—
and the child's tooth loosens
and her father ties a sheer string
around the doorknob, shuts the door fast,
so she holds what was once
part of her in the palm of her hand.

Tethering the Ocean Swells

I am not the woman I followed in London
who filled her stolen grocery cart with cans
of cat food and steered it to the park.

I still have hope that before long
I'll find a four-leaf clover and paste it
right here in the pages of my journal,

that when I go to the optometrist,
the "D-E-F-P-O-T" on the Snellen chart
will no longer sway like a boat on open sea,

that I will answer correctly
when asked, which hologram fly
pops up closest to me.

On the corner, last Saturday at five,
a man was polishing the brass
handrails at the Baptist church.

He moved his rag so evenly
I thought I might sneak up
the marble steps and hold him.

But now, I am afraid he just went home
and fixed himself a frozen dinner
looking out on the street below.

Magic Show

The child nimbly holds a sparkler of light,
share of brightness, like a parcel of land,
so what matters most becomes effortless,
trailing her in the low meadow at dusk.

You can change a person's life
by saying just one thing, just once.

It is the fourth of July, and off in the distance
older children, insistent as shadows,
call for the fireworks to begin.
Who is she that light will stay with her?

A Greek chorus moves together so as to
be believed as one, everything in song.

At home, her mother draws water
into the cast iron tub, holds her hand
under the faucet, still for one brief moment
as she has not let herself be before.

In the field, the fireworks have begun.
But this part of the story you already know.

She takes a hydrangea blossom, the brightest
blue, drapes petals all over the porch
facing Little Flattop Mountain,
and puts on a magic show, lighter than their frailty.

A shadow stays with us even when there is light.
See your shadow? See mine?

II
Stillness

Field Guide to Stillness

There is a steep hill and clover
thick as lamb's ear, as leather bellows
splayed to rouse fire embers.
And there is a boy lying motionless
at the hill's crest waiting
for the right moment to roll
unencumbered to the meadow
which parallels the creek.

In his mind the knowing
of what it is to fly.

In his mind such longing.
Nightfall. Daybreak.

But this particular boy
will let himself go
so he can rest
near the water invisible
smell of sassafras close
in the air, so he can think
of the imaginary bridge
he keeps on drawing,
of his picture of the wind.

And This Shall Be a Sign Unto You

It may not sound like much, but all spring
I've looked for something that could tell me
what I've done is right, sign unblemished
as a peony's sheer petals, my daughter's legs
as she pumps on the playground swing set,
rising lighter and nimbler in the afternoon air.

There's an open sunlit room, and I am practicing
to lie like a corpse, hold still enough
so as to be what I must become.
There are different ways to think about this:
when a black snake sheds, its skin is yellow.
A mare's withers shudder even though
it has been moments since the fly alighted.

This particular morning I need to see
if I can make the shape of what was once there,
the way on plywood pegboard an indelible marker
draws out a hammer's outline so the shape
will be recognizable even when the tool is not.

But metaphor is, of course, a willed error,
and so I've driven to Concrete World
to buy a statue angel for the garden.
I tell myself this has got to work.
This has got to be what I'm looking for.
But there's a ladder on the roof
of the warehouse and no sign
of lines being chalked or shingles nailed.
Maybe I should begin to see
that what I ask is not easy.
Blink your eyes, see what happens.

Catalogue of Silence

There's a new foal in the field beside the road,
and when I drive by, he is pacing back and forth
looking for something he will never find.

Next door, children skate on February ice, circling
each other in paths swept clean of snow.

In the middle ages, all the hours of the day, monks bent
over velum, illuminating the Bible: each "E"
curly as a ram's horn, "O" holding dominion

over the parable as if to say there is nothing
more wild than a mouth open in awe.

O, Once upon a time there was a mime,
and each door he closed never made a sound
even though he did it all the days of his life.

In the Other Room My Daughter
Plays with Her Dollhouse

To start with, there's a stillness
to it, even the way she speaks
to the dolls, assuring them it's not
going to rain after all.

She moves them, room to room.

I can hear the *tap tap* of one
walking up the wooden stairs,
picture in my mind how it works
the way you picture roots
pushing sturdily into black earth.
By now she's forgotten
I'm anywhere at all,
even deeper and quieter than sleep,
than the blue-eyed grasses
that close at nightfall,
moon so bright I can see clear
to the sycamore at the end
of the drive where there's
a nest balanced high
in the peeling branches.

I once had a fish
and watched it arch up
to the pieces of food floating.
I thought it could be gold,
thought of someplace far away,
of what it sounds like
when steam rises
from the blacktop.

Underneath the Hot Air Balloons

It begins with how mutely
they float, deeper and further
into obscurity, how
the passengers' hearts
must lift the way they do
on narrow county roads.

The train looks so small
in morning fog,
and the old sycamores
by the creek:
they are pale as talcum.

This is the world being poured
into a bowl, gentle as the elephant
who shoves his box
across smooth concrete
in tender starts,
curious as the worlds
children make, holding
their breaths under water:

if he hollers
let him go,
and you
are it.

Exactitude

I dig in the dirt under stalks of forsythia
my mother wants to tear out,
pull away stones, create a world
so I can see inside myself,
build something that has not been before,
thin stick nicking shape from black earth,
world tiny and ingenious as Calder's circus
whose tightrope walkers balance in midair.
I am doing what he did as his wife wound
the gramophone, Calder's enormous,
tender hands shuffling acrobats in the ring.
I will make something accurate as a mobile
swinging across the ceiling casting
ruby and cobalt light,
as bevel clusters in the windows
of Saint Christopher's by the Sea.

Did I say something too sudden?
This must be what Mandelstam meant
by the words *ordinary heartbreak*.

My Daughter's First Day of School

She is singing, but I can't hear her
nor the red-topped hay fields
that pass by the school bus
even though their incandescence
is itself a song, recurrent and jubilant
as the quivering of crickets
rising up in the August air.

This time it is me in danger of falling:
you can look in the creek's water,
see rocks, but there's part of them
not really there, at least not
in a way you can depend on anymore.

All night the melody of the ice cream truck
threads over the still alleys. All day
my daughter in the window of the school bus
singing a song I will never know.

Stablehand's Song

Today, in the fields, the season's last cutting: square bales.
My German neighbor and his son
stand for a moment in the stillness
seeing the barn loft where they're going
to stack the hay in layers so exact,
one across another, horizontal then vertical,
not even the wind will unfasten this work they've done.

Come January, evening feeding out, shafts of sun
seeping through slats in the high barn, they'll reach
gloved hands and remember this October light,
shimmering of rust on the mountainside,
they'll grasp bailing twine holding sweet clover.

In a week's time there will be a rain so heavy as to fill
the creek, raising it over the banks of the rutted road.

But how do you fully imagine a subject for yourself?
Think about going underground: wouldn't it be pitch black?
Think of birds' bones, hollow, filled with air
so they can drift away, right up in the sky.

My neighbor's wife became
so used to the swaying of the ship
she felt the rocking weeks after,
even though she'd sworn
never to see the ocean again.

There were horses on the ferry
to the mainland. They couldn't get
their footing, wanted to lie down.
But their halters kept them up,
tethered to the sides of the trailer.

I was there, my job to keep them calm,
twist the twitch around their muzzle so tight
I couldn't look in their eyes where fear of the ferry's
shifts mounted perilous as floodwater.

How to Claim Silence

When you say to me, *I believe,*
it holds much power.
But the mind wanders
more readily than the body.
That's why the coon dog,
bone tired, circles
the coil rug over and over,
steadying her mind.
Orchard blossoms
piteously bright,
I have the urge to climb
the ladder, wrap my hands
round the top rung,
let go with my feet.
Let's say it
this way: in the East,
if you circumambulate
a sacred place,
you acquire merit.
I pace around my mother
as she reads in her wingchair,
making of the rug's perimeter
a balance beam, following
the flower pattern as it passes,
waiting for something
she is never going to say.

Silent Duet

In the auditorium, the signer's hands flutter
so if they were glass they'd be the sun catcher
in my daughter's window,
upper field at first light after hard frost.
I watch them float, etch out what the rest of us hear,
do this for a woman two rows in front of me
who looks not at him, but beyond, to the brambles
where last night she flushed a covey of quail so sudden
the birds rose up speckling the air,
scattering sparks like a mountain on fire.
She felt them quiver out of the underbrush.

The signer enfolds himself, holds his own body.
And who can say there is anything more we need?
I want to be her, the silent way snow makes the world.
And these birds, this man who loves her enough to beckon
what, for the rest of us, has been uttered and let go.
Like water in the Roman baths, considered royal
because it once surged through the emperor's aqueducts,
his hands are tethered to the sky
as he draws the words this way for her.
In morning's light, she's smaller than her own shadow.
Her eyes see two worlds at once.

To the Men Who Mow the County Graveyards

It won't be long before the designs you form are echoed
in the shivering leaves of an ash tree right there on the hillside

and because it's November they will remain
all winter long, a sort of engraved, emblazoned pattern.

You are walking cautiously and must be able
to read the stones: *Earth hath no sorrow heaven cannot heal.*

Robert Morris, Garland Maupin, Jacob Hall
who just this spring whacked at the bull thistle in his clover field

with a steel scythe, timbre so sheer I held my breath,
as I did, once, under water, because the clang of an anchor

resounded in the heavy sea and my whole body
unwrapped right there in the harbor.

Look back over your shoulder.
The grass is gently sweeping like water at your feet.

It's the same lustrous quiet as the time Robert held
the black string of his dousing pendulum over a plat of land.

At first he whispered, then was wordless, balancing the lead
teardrop between thumb and index finger, letting it sway

and sway in shorter and shorter arcs.
Watching him I felt I'd come a little more alive.

In the dusk somewhere tonight a table lamp comes on.
A woman sits under it recognizing, suddenly, she is all alone.

There is a river moving under all the land.
There never was a night that had no morn.

III
Confinement

Field Guide to Confinement

Tell me when you don't remember
the exact way your sister interlocked
her hands at the dinner table, half listening
to the talk of adults whose lives were
distant as winter flounder motionless
on mud flats or if you no longer recall
how layers of onion on the wood
cutting board refused to unpeel
the way you'd allowed them to in your dream.
Maybe all I fear is not going to come true.
Maybe no one's missing after all.
Except, more often than not,
long winter shadows gouge crevices
into my neighbor's cedar,
and I'm afraid to show him what I see.
Think of Jonah caged three whole days
in the belly of a whale
and still, he lived to tell about it.

Flip Book

Once a fire moves away from you,
it is not coming back, grass and brush

burned, leaving only earth to smolder
the way mist in the early morning

billows close over the reservoir
when the water is warmer than air.

The water is not a field,
even though I see it that way.

When we were little, Clark and I
made book movies. On the first page

we'd draw a cat. On the next, the same
cat with its paw one inch forward, then two,

so when you flipped fast, the cat stalked
across the book. We did this in secret,

upstairs, where our mother wouldn't see
we wanted something she couldn't give us

as the attic windows let in
summer light at an angle all around.

After dark, after all the children
have been called home and the Labrador

circles his canvas bed, after traffic lights
switch to nighttime blinking, she will move

between the rooms of the house looking
for something she cannot find,

looking for what is familiar
like how to ride a bike or skate

effortlessly across a frozen pond.

Prayer List

My neighbor keeps a list of people
to pray for above the kitchen sink,
so when she's doing dishes
she'll think of them, eyes closed as she ploughs
her hands through sudsy water, reaching
for the plate whose rose design has dulled.

There is a place inside me that remembers
more than it should, and in a way I cannot
explain to anyone at all. Now when I dream
of my mother's death, she is following
a prescribed regimen, each day swallowing
a bright red pill that brings her closer to the end.

Last night I called my childhood best friend.
She's in love with a lobsterman.
They'll marry in the fall when waves
break against the harbor pilings.
But don't you see?
My mother did not want to stop the dying.

The Art of Escape

The passenger train runs parallel
to the road for over a mile,
but still, I cannot see the faces.
In the storybook the boy grows
wings, gradually, as if he might
get accustomed to that, too, the way
he did his father's absence after the war.
The elevator inspector slides his initials
under glass, remembering, the whole time,
how the deepest trips are to the mines.

First Star I See Tonight

There was a winter bird I couldn't name.
I lay under the snow and it sang,
invisible wire from its filled chest
to my head which was cradled
by what the child had packed
so dutifully around me.

But here's what's worse:
that night I couldn't find
the little girl in the apartment house
where she and her mother lived.
I called *Mattie* all up and down
the long hallways until the name
took on a hard sound and so I stopped.

Then someone slammed a door
and there was silence.

This is when I remembered
the time it was too wet to work
the garden and I knelt beside
the red soil, patted some with my hands,
hoping if I waited long enough
I'd be able to change things after all.
Above me two tulip poplars
molted their tranquil stars
and so I looked up—
wish I may, wish I might.

When I found the child
she'd carefully wedged
her body into a guitar case.
How well she fit
in that empty, velvet box.

Making a Thunderstorm

When it rained for days
we'd crowd in the dining hall:
a long, wooden building
with screens for windows
so the water from the roof
sounded closer like it was
inside where we were.
As the afternoon wore on
and the counselors came back
from wherever they'd gone
to talk or smoke or call someone,
they arranged us in lines
along the benches
and we made a thunderstorm.
The first in line would rub
her hands together and the next
and the next until a loud shushing
filled the room, the soft rain.
Then we'd snap our fingers,
one and the next and the next
until the heavier rain was coming.
And when we clapped our hands
the rain soared forceful over the mountain.
In August, when I get home,
the house will feel empty
without all the other children.
When I tell my mother about the storms,
she will nod, and it will be the same
as her humming when she drives
or whistling behind her teeth
when she has heard bad news.

Hand Shadows on a Wall

Jacob knows where the moon is,
even if it's risen far too early
a winter afternoon, risen the color
of storm clouds, of motionlessness.

He sees it in town, at Settle Tire
when he rolls a rim out to the trash pile.

Sees it alone in lamplight where he entwines
his fingers to make a goose, a gander,
a perfect rabbit on the wall.

In his mind the war again, and he's
hoisting signal flags from the halyard,
shapes so plain they must be warning:

Keep well clear at slow speed.
I am on fire.

But he is the only one who is his voice,
who feels the quiet like a fever pass
through him or the world become pale,
years that follow one another and never
a way to catch himself in time.

This is not about the moment
he found the missing boy skipping stones
in the creek or the way wind divides
the hillside grass in flawless waves.

Before his shadow bird takes wing
he'll think up words his mother

would say, slow as the unerring moon
climbs her window as the found boy throws
his final round of hopscotch in the new dark.

Below him, daysleepers rise,
readying for the night.

He moves his bed so the headboard faces
her room and the backyard
where he's placed a stick in the storm drain
so this snow, when it melts,
will at least have somewhere to go.

Readying for the Storm

At the naval yard,
before the hurricane,
ships are put to open sea
where they rock as dark
clouds build in the east,
strange as the dream
of standing so small
in sunlight listening
to the dull sound
of the neighbor's mower
in the long backyard
that juts from his house.
At the public park
swings have been looped
over the steel bars.
There they are,
guarded against the wind,
and all the boats,
the supply ships and frigates,
mine sweeps and tankers,
sway like a person standing
in line holding a child.
Out in the rising storm
ships cannot come to harm
against the piers, the wharves.
Think of a tree felled:
it's already lying down.

The Cancer Patient Dreams

This is the underside of the world
delicate and transparent as ice,
as maple leaves red as heat,
the very ones she raked this morning,
the ones strewn all over the yard,
so the made piles rattle
the exact moment
the train goes by, carrying coal
from the mountains eastward.
She turns and goes inside,
sweeps her room in the dark,
hoping for an alchemist,
someone to change lead into gold.

For the Hospital Staff

It was better when they were in the room,
shuffle of charts and arranging of sheets.
Late in the morning a nurse came
to put in a catheter, carefully threading
the needle with thick navy floss.
He looked so completely sure
what he was doing was right, my hands let go
of the chair they had stiffened on for hours.
I thought of this today, driving home.
By November you can see far in the woods
squinting through bare trees to remember
a stone chimney or abandoned cabin,
houses you'd even forgotten were there.
She would have loved this: driving the dirt
roads as the light falls behind Flattop Mountain.
In the country you hear a truck
long before it comes into sight;
that way you can imagine who it is
and think of what you might have to say to them.

In the Movies

A ghost can step through
glass even while holding an actual object.
This, of course, defies logic
and is why we remember it:
so otherworldly yet utterly real.
Like this morning at the grocery store
after treatment when I hear
the girl at checkout
ask if the cilantro is parsley,
and I remember being nine again,
hiding in the tall grass waiting,
it's August by the lake, and voices across
the way have become so faint
as to be sound without meaning.

In optical art, the negative afterimage
is what matters most: all those contiguous
black boxes pulsating seconds
after you've turned your eyes away.
When you have cancer, what makes
people whisper is what's too real to see.
Don't worry: I'm here in the summer grass
pretending to be covered with snow
so cold it blazes in mid-afternoon sun.

IV
Vanishing

Field Guide to Vanishing

In fifth grade Edith Pepper went
every afternoon for swallowing lessons.
And because she'd leave class early
and because my desk was next to hers,
I kept seeing her in a straight back chair
in the downtown doctor's office.
The nurse must have asked her to curve
her tongue to the roof of her mouth
the very moment the outbound bus sighed
at the corner stop. She must have thought
of us still staring at the globe our teacher
so valiantly held, pointing out places
where it was an entirely different day.

On the news, this autumn, always a flood,
waters rising over houses and graves.
So I take my daughter to the railroad tracks
to gather stray spikes for sharing at school.
Yesterday as we paced the timber crossties,
so redolent with creosote, the mountains
to the west began moving as summer's
green gave rise to the purpling sumac.

Like you, I'm wishing to change things,
wishing for some place far away.
Picture the octopus: when it wants to hide,
it just lets go a cloud of dark black ink.

Night Writing

I'm going to paint and make it the evening,
the light under the eaves, the motionless air,
teach myself to say this the right way
because if I don't it's entirely probable
the night world, dimmer than mottled
apple leaves, will pass through me.

I want to make the grass on the mountain
autumn red, send my love a box of leaves
so he'll see them lifted from the ground,
color intensified the way bent metal
shimmers at the crease or the way two doves
on the electric line are suspended
more nimbly than if they sat on a plain limb.

I recognize the danger in trying
to shape what isn't there.

And while there are words I'd never use—
shame, for instance, its *sssh* sound
so like how we shush a child—
I have the feeling something crucial
and exalted is needed to change
what I've been fearing, now, for days.

Watching by the Window

In almost every species of bird, the male
is more colorful: glossy blue black
woodpecker, chestnut yellow warbler.
It is okay, writing that here.
But when I think of it, of the female
so ordinary, finch and vireo alike,
I remember the years I remained invisible
so as not to ask for anything at all.
In the meadow this morning
a house wren floated over cut hay
and the faintness of her, like a canopy
of gauze, disappeared into thin air.

Not Telling Anything New

You probably know
this is a box of gold,
woman throwing ashes
on the turned garden,
the snow that comes down,
wind soughing the meadow.

I am trying to see things as they are
but the moon might disappear
while you are looking, the ocean
cease to dwell in the sea
glass you hold.

I was afraid of losing him
and it happened.

Leaves decompose
in water the rain left,
tiny punched holes
elaborate as lace.

The only way I know
how to say this
is still not right.

I saw a bird carry her daughter
over the Great Strand River.

It gets cold. It gets dark.

There are bright specks on the snow.
Come, quick, before they fly away.

Rehearsal for the Real Thing

When I went to shovel out the barn, the creased door
slammed in wind, not even startling Melvin
who has thought all this through,
such a hunger to see things the way he used to,
singing, sometimes, under his breath so you
can be sure it's risen in his head.

Here is not my place.
I could have told you that long ago.

This morning it's *Bye Bye Blackbird*,
and suddenly the sun so bright
I begin to undress, wind shifting
through fields of broomsedge.

I fell in love with the rain,
all Sunday last aching for it.
See how alike those two wishes are?

This is going to be a song about leaving,
seven o'clock, nightfall, lit highway trucks
swishing into distance.

All the water that is rain
once came out of the ground
where my neighbor walks his fence line,
tenderly circling the field
until I can't say anymore
why this touches me so.
Water boils on the cast iron stove.

Behind the chipped paint of the station
walls, a woman in brown stares
blankly at her baby, legs tucked
under her in the half dark even
as she's thinking about her grandmother
taking laudanum, cheaper than gin.
She has to do what she can,
this smell of her childhood apartment
house where always a child is crying,
always something unnamable
until, one day, she's older
than she ever imagined she ever would be.

So the Snow Will Fall this Night

I mean this poem
to be a magic spell
because for now
only cold rain falls.
Cows kneel
beside the dark pond
that hides
summer's snapping turtle.
They pull at late grass,
kneel the way a child does
listening to this story
his teacher holds,
tendril of a world far away.

Volunteering in the Kindergarten Classroom

The teacher has spread huge pieces
of ivory paper on the linoleum
where the children lie down,
quiet as dusk, to have their bodies traced.

They are so still I want to show them
the blue heron who just this morning
hovered above the creek's high water,
then set sail over the freshened fields.

They will see their breath in winter,
hear torrents of rain on the roof,
taste the ocean's metal, smell
the gleaming fire in the burn pile.

Victoria turns her head
to tell William of all the places
in the world she has been.
It's enough to make you love most anything.

Later she shows me her drawings:
That's the sound of an owl.
That's my fish in water.
That's me, even when I'm not really here.

Child's Question on a Chalkboard

Why is it
when you stand
outside
very still
without any
clothes on
you can't feel
the world moving?

All the Day Through

I play clapping games in line at the cafeteria
with Della whose father drank cyanide
up behind the barn two Thursdays past,
drank at dusk so no one could find
him until it was too late.

At school we're learning songs:
Oh how lovely is the evening.
And facts: how when the British
rounded the Cape of Good Hope
they felt such promise in the tepid water
until goods perished in the ships' hulls.

Helium's lighter than air,
water weighs more than petroleum
and the moon pulls at the tide.

But Della's only thinking of her father.
She's singing under her breath:
she jumped so high, she reached the sky.

So for Della I paint cows
chewing their cud in the sun,
sturdy jaws circling, teeth pulling
clover at an angle, tearing it away.

There's nothing I can do
that will change things.
Della must wake up alone,
with only the shape of her own body,
and the light outside which is softer
because it's getting to be autumn
and she'll feel this all so much more.

Catalogue of the Unseen

The man in line next to me
is named Thomas, like my father,
and when I hear him say it
something inside almost floats
the way watching hurricane coverage
you can believe
there resides a mystery
just out of reach.
Why else would the reporters stand
like that in the devouring wind,
bright yellow coats flapping
so like the siding that will loosen
once the storm finally hits?
And now, deep winter,
days as short as ever they'll be,
I so plainly feel alarm.
Even the prospect of a phone call
has me wishing I could vanish
and do it dispassionately
so no one could tell
I'd ever been here.

I understood this all
so differently as a child.
The one time I ran away
and hid behind the neighbor's
pink azalea, I was not
for one moment doubtful
someone would find me.

There is a downed tree
along the county road

heading west.
Each spring it blooms
this white so indelible
it leaves streaks in your eyes
like a photograph of the stars
when long exposure reveals trails
as earth turns under our sky
catching what is moving,
what we cannot see.

Negative Space

First I am going to make the sea sturdy
and shameless as the body of a bird,
filled with such splendor nothing cruel
can weave itself in her stirring waters.

Next I will draw a moth that flies,
but can also, if need be, settle itself:
over there, for instance, on the stone wall
that steadies the wild grasses growing nearby.

Then I will splay the moth's
wings and because their color
is velvet, that surrender
will have a certain majesty.

One night I swam far out in the lake
way past where buoys marked
lines in the mountain water.
For awhile I held my breath
so not even my own breathing
would distract me.

It was, it turned out,
the only thing I wanted.

This is the same as learning
to draw the spaces between the clouds,
like learning to see what isn't there
which is, finally, what some of us really want.

V
Dreaming

Field Guide to Dreaming

Even though it is night
and the moss by the wellhead
knows such stillness as the sound
doves make, a boy is sung to sleep,
dreams three brothers are unloading
ice at Saul's Mercantile.
His body shifts each time
another layer is peeled
from the truck's bed,
each time closer to the hard place
in his heart he cannot clothe.
How the single bags soar
for a moment between brothers' hands
only to be shut again in a frozen borough,
how everything gradually
turns back to what it first was.

But suddenly his mother's eyes
are feathers, uncontained as the ocean,
unmistakable as the harvest moon.

She is picking apples,
showing him to look for magic
or a cloud that can drape itself
so intentionally over the adjacent hillside,
the cattle pastured there
are enveloped in a furlong of shade.

What Makes It Still Winter

A ballet is a story hid
in a book under a bed.
But don't you see:
she wants to be something else,
stick that floats far from shore
above the penitent river
or a sign, a memorized fairy tale.

The postman gives her a letter,
and she gets to go away,
be a girl in a glass dress.

What is it to be alive?
A thing asking mercy?

That's why I'm saying this to you:
so the night won't seem as long.

It's raining now.

Under the eaves the sound echoes

And look—
how beautiful is the water:
anything but what it is.

The heart floats.

The light on the cows,
glory like the scatter rug
your grandfather laid before the hearth.

Tell Yourself a Story

To fall asleep make lists:
who you saw at the grocery,
what books are due at the library.
This is how to become
tired enough.

    Or remember how the fields
    have texture like corduroy.
    In one direction
    run furrows of the plough,
    in another, red top hay
    mottled as linen.

Go to the window
over the street where cars
are parked up close to the curb
to look out at the corner,
the few stars overhead.

    In the pasture three chestnut
    horses wear masks of netting
    so the grass at their hooves looks
    fractured as graph paper.
    At dusk they must be half blind.

Soon a friend will come to visit
so you can drive to where people
sit out Sunday afternoon
on their porches,
not even talking.
Tell yourself *at least I'm trying.*

Beside the field there's
a new fence of woven wire
in perfect squares,
the creek's shadowless water
layered with leaves.

Evensong

This is the night
he'll hear something
like a bat whirring
through the barn rafters
so he can become
a little more who he is,
the water the rain left
pooled beside him,
the branches that shift,
the moon's light flickering.

For many nights I watch him
from the window,
lean my elbows on the sill
so it is I who become
a statue after all.

I'm waiting for the woodcock
to flutter over the meadow
to tell me it's morning,
have to wake
the child every hour,
keep the concussion
from taking hold.
She tripped in the sweet fern,
hit her head while we walked
the ridge gathering windfall.
The freight train had passed by
and we couldn't hear each other
for more time than I can say.

I want to be made of air
so I can float over
the sodden meadow,
make the morning come.

Silhouette

Truckers sleep in their cabs by the roadside, swathed
in lightless inches, half-hearing the whoosh of traffic

heading east to the ocean, while deep in the crepe myrtle
six songbirds nest. But this is a dream about a place

I've never been. There is a boy dressed like a ghost
standing in the light. He wants to be more himself,

more transparent, wishes, for one moment,
someone will recognize him for who he is.

Above his parents' bed hangs "Christina's World,"
grass around the distant house and barn mown with such care

that if she could reach it, leaning, as she does, on slender
wrists, the very deftness of its being shorn would give

her hope. The painting's browns sing under their breath
just like birds out in the leaves the whole morning long,

sing for the boy, sealed in the house, who
becomes no different from the light.

A Little More to Hold Onto

This is a painting of a woman
stepping out of the bath,
softened foot lifted same
as light on the cows in the field.

She knows not to fly away.

In her mind the moon is moving.
But it's only clouds shuttering the beam.

There are things that still matter in our lives:
children paring their names in hardening concrete,
leaning watchfully, the click of branches
their small hands hold, wetness rising.

Maybe that's what I meant to say after all.

The other story's strange
as the locusts who'll
come again this year.

Magic is real, you know:
the body of the mind.

The woman's still in the bath
and in no danger of falling.
She's left the windows smudged
for sparrows who'd otherwise
fly straight into them.

Divination

I dream I'm still in school,
but all the other children have gone
home so it's quiet enough

to hear the silences between the sounds,
picture the three bones that float
in the body, not resting on anything at all.

My sister told me so, even before
she pressed a pear on her swollen belly,
and the baby, when it was born

had that exact shape,
the color of salmon, right
in the center of her brow.

What's burning inside me is hard to define.
All I do is look up, there in the trees:
winter mistletoe lives on nothing but air.

What's Being Counted and Why

Hannah said the answer before I could.
She's the pastor's grandchild
so her words stretch far,
like my mother talking
to someone who's not even here.

The story starts this way:
there's a votive candle
in the shadowy nave
I'm hoping might bring her back,
same as the far-off light
grown real as water the rain left
or the whirling Grumman prop
you see only in a photograph.

Birds cluster this winter morning.
Horses sleep standing in their stalls.

Bats time their sounds so
the echoes tell them where objects are.
Counting his breath in the cold,
a boy waits in shadow for me,
rises up bright as the night moth
arcing over the houses of sleepers
nimble as fish who burrow
in the dark bottom of the sea.

Pasture Roses

The spell I'm under has little to do with how they drape
disruptively over the fence or even how the rails form
exact hexagons. Last night's wind came sudden
churning the small fires built to stave off first frost.

Flickering, buoyant plumes rose high in the vineyard air.
This is when the fragile roses crossed themselves, and in
their shadows were the shapes of animals. I watched them
very closely. My grandmother tacked a sheet to the wall

and, with her hands, made a snail, a moose, the farmer in the dell.
But that was years ago. This time the shapes really exist.
I've put water in a galvanized basin and the stick
lying so still at the bottom is, without warning, irrefutably bent.

Still Life Action Movie

My heart is pounding through my chest,
and my shining limbs are shaken beneath me.
—The Iliad

The girl's hands pick
up speed as if she's
directing traffic or a small
orchestra, but no one's really there,
so the men standing idle in the street
let her watch their wish for rain,
hear them talk of the grey fox
who lives with her family
under the sea wall at night.
She can be that other person
for now, the boy she wanted
to switch places with.
But when the funeral home
explains that what she'll get
in the urn will be someone
else along with her mother,
and less of her mother,
she no longer wants
what she did before.
It's suddenly cold
and the men have gone home.
Not five miles away
a storm mounts, and all the leaves
she'd collected for the fox's den
disintegrate just like that.

Days That Haven't Happened Yet

The day after my mother died, I called
her answering machine to tape her voice.
I didn't know what else to do,
tenor so lush no other human being
could match the things she said.
She could make a sound like some birds,
or pause, mid-sentence, so you'd be sure
what was to come would change things.

She was only half there much of the time.
Like the boy at the doctor's office
who flapped his arms singing
"butterfly, butterfly" as June's light
ruptured the waiting room floor,
who kept on singing, a living thing relieved
to be other than what he was.

In another city, my friend sleeps
a sleep from which she'll never rise.
The bones of a leaf hold up flesh.
I want her to dream she's flying
in a field somewhere she'll find
what she's suspected all along:
that she is two beings at once.

About the Book

Type designer Eric Gill's most popular Roman typeface is Perpetua, which was released by the Monotype Corporation between 1925 and 1932. It first appeared in a limited edition of the book *The Passion of Perpetua and Felicity*, for which the typeface was named. The italic form was originally called Felicity. Perpetua's clean chiseled look recalls Gill's stonecutting work and makes it an excellent text typeface, giving sparkle to long passages of text; the Perpetua capitals have beautiful, classical lines that make this one of the finest display alphabets available.

Cover Photo by John Gould

Design by Robert B. Cumming, Jr.

Charlotte Matthews is the author of one previous full length collection of poetry, *Green Stars* (Iris Press, 2006). She is also the author of two chapbooks, *A Kind of Devotion* (Palanquin Press, 2004) and *Biding Time* (Half Moon Bay Press, 2005). Her work has appeared in *The Virginia Quarterly Review, Borderlands, Ecotone, Tar River Poetry,* and *storySouth*. Most recently she received the 2007 New Writers Award from the Fellowship for Southern Writers. She is a graduate of The University of Virginia and The MFA Program for Writers at Warren Wilson College. She teaches in the Bachelor of Interdisciplinary and Professional Studies at the University of Virginia.

Printed in the United States
109408LV00001B/197/A

9 780916 078843